To:

_____

From:

_____

Date:

_____

Love Never Fails

© 2010 Summerside Press™

www.summersidepress.com

ISBN 978-1-935416-92-0

Designed by Lisa & Jeff Franke.

Summerside Press™ is an inspirational publisher offering fresh, irresistible books to uplift the heart and engage the mind.

Printed in the USA.

Love Never Fails
A Pocket Inspirations Book

summerside
PRESS

Tenderly Loved

What inexpressible joy for me,
to look up through the apple blossoms
and the fluttering leaves,
and to see God's love there;
to listen to the thrush
that has built his nest among them,
and to feel God's love,
who cares for the birds,
in every note that swells his little throat;
to look beyond to the bright blue depths of the sky,
and feel they are a canopy of blessing–
the roof of the house of my Father.

ELIZABETH RUNDELL CHARLES

I have loved you with an everlasting love;
I have drawn you with loving-kindness.

JEREMIAH 31:3 NIV

We are so preciously loved by God that we cannot
even comprehend it. No created being
can ever know how much and how sweetly
and tenderly God loves them. It is only with
the help of His grace that we are able to
persevere in...endless wonder at the high,
surpassing, immeasurable love which our
Lord in His goodness has for us.

JULIAN OF NORWICH

Sincere Love

Sooner or later, we begin to understand that love
is more than verses on valentines and romance in
the movies. We begin to know that love is here and
now, real and true, the most important thing in our
lives. For love is the creator of our favorite memories
and the foundation of our fondest dreams.
Love is a promise that is always kept, a fortune
that can never be spent, a seed that can flourish
in even the most unlikely of places. And this radiance
that never fades, this mysterious and magical
joy, is the greatest treasure of all—one known
only by those who love.

When we really love others, we accept them as they
are. We make our love visible through little acts of
kindness, shared activities, words of praise and thanks,
and our willingness to get along with them.

EDWARD E. FORD

*L*ove makes all labor light. We serve
with enthusiasm where we love with sincerity.

HANNAH MORE

*D*on't just pretend to love others.
Really love them....

ROMANS 12:9–10 NLT

*W*hen the heart is pure it cannot help
loving, because it has discovered the
source of love, which is God.

JEAN-MARIE BAPTISTE VIANNEY

Love Is...

I may speak in different languages of people or even angels. But if I do not have love, I am only a noisy bell or a crashing cymbal. I may have the gift of prophecy. I may understand all the secret things of God and have all knowledge, and I may have faith so great I can move mountains. But even with all these things, if I do not have love, then I am nothing. I may give away everything I have, and I may even give my body as an offering to be burned. But I gain nothing if I do not have love. Love is patient and kind. Love is not jealous, it does not brag, and it is not proud. Love is not rude, is not selfish, and does not get upset with others. Love does not count up wrongs that have been done. Love takes no pleasure in evil but rejoices over the truth. Love patiently accepts all things. It always trusts, always hopes, and always endures. Love never ends.

1 CORINTHIANS 13:1–8 NCV

*L*ove Him totally who gave Himself
totally for your love.

*C*LARE OF *A*SSISI

*Y*ou, O God, are both tender and kind,
not easily angered, immense in love,
and you never, never quit.

*P*SALM 86:15 THE MESSAGE

*L*ove *is a fruit in season at all times,*
and within the reach of every hand.

*M*OTHER *T*ERESA

Love Beyond Words

True love possesses the ability to see beyond. In that
sense we might say that love has X-ray vision. It goes
beyond mere words. It sees beneath the veneer. Love
focuses on the soul. Love sees another's soul in great
need of help and sets compassion to work.

CHARLES SWINDOLL

True gratitude, like true love,
must find expression in acts, not words.

R. MILDRED BARKER

All the beautiful sentiments in the world
weigh less than a simple lovely action.

JAMES RUSSELL LOWELL

A good deed is never lost; he who sows courtesy reaps
friendship, and he who plants kindness gathers love.

BASIL OF CAESAREA

Love is an action—it means doing, serving, giving.

PAT WILLIAMS

I am praying that you will put into action the generosity that comes from your faith as you understand and experience all the good things we have in Christ.

PHILEMON 1:6 NLT

Our greatness rests solely on the fact that God in His incomprehensible goodness has bestowed His love upon us. God does not love us because we are so valuable; we are valuable because God loves us.

HELMUT THIELICKE

Live God's Way

It is obvious what kind of life develops out of trying to get your own way all the time: repetitive, loveless, cheap sex...emotional garbage; frenzied and joyless grabs for happiness...all-consuming-yet-never-satisfied wants; a brutal temper; an impotence to love or be loved; divided homes and divided lives; small-minded and lopsided pursuits...uncontrolled and uncontrollable addictions.... I could go on.... If you use your freedom this way, you will not inherit God's kingdom.
But what happens when we live God's way? He brings gifts into our lives, much the same way that fruit appears in an orchard—things like affection for others, exuberance about life, serenity. We develop a willingness to stick with things, a sense of compassion in the heart, and a conviction that a basic holiness permeates things and people. We find ourselves involved in loyal commitments, not needing to force our way in life, able to marshal and direct our energies wisely.

GALATIANS 5:19–23 THE MESSAGE

*W*e prove ourselves by our purity,
our understanding,
our patience, our kindness,
by the Holy Spirit within us,
and by our sincere love.

2 CORINTHIANS 6:6 NLT

If God is not lost in our lives,
if goodness is not lost in our lives,
if memories are not lost in our lives,
then we will have an easier time
of finding our way to personal happiness.

CHRISTOPHER DE VINCK

Fulfilling Our Desire

God is not only the answer to a thousand needs,
He is the answer to a thousand wants.
He is the fulfillment of our chief desire in all of life.
For whether or not we've ever recognized it,
what we desire is unfailing love.
Oh, God, awake our souls to see—
You are what we want, not just what we need.
Yes, our life's protection,
but also our heart's affection.
Yes, our soul's salvation,
but also our heart's exhilaration.
Unfailing love. A love that will not let me go!

BETH MOORE

God is every moment totally aware of each one of us.
Totally aware in intense concentration and love....
No one passes through any area of life, happy
or tragic, without the attention of God with him.

EUGENIA PRICE

*G*od will generously provide all you need.
Then you will always have everything you
need and plenty left over to share with others....
Yes, you will be enriched in every
way so that you can always be generous.

2 CORINTHIANS 9:8, 11 NLT

*W*e desire many things, and God offers
us only one thing. He can offer us only one thing—
Himself. He has nothing else to give.
There is nothing else to give.

PETER KREEFT

Say It with Love

If there's something you need to say to your
loved one, remember to say it lovingly,
as if holding his heart in your hands.

ELLEN SUE STERN

Let everything you say be good and helpful,
so that your words will be an encouragement
to those who hear them.... Be kind to each other,
tenderhearted, forgiving one another,
just as God through Christ has forgiven you.

EPHESIANS 4:29, 32 NLT

Kindness is tenderness, kindness is love....
Kindness comes very close to the benevolence of God.

RANDOLPH RAY

Let yours be a mind through which Christ thinks,
a heart through which Christ loves,
a voice through which Christ speaks,
a hand through which Christ helps.

$\mathcal{W}$alk softly. Speak tenderly. Love fervently.

$\mathcal{S}$o in everything, do to others what you
would have them do to you, for this
sums up the Law and the Prophets.

$\mathcal{M}$ATTHEW 7:12 NIV

$\mathcal{L}$ord, help me to spread Your fragrance
everywhere I go, and may Your radiant
light be visible through me.

Pay It Forward

The greatest thing...a person can do for his
or her heavenly Father is to be kind to some
of His other children.

I wonder why it is we are not all kinder than we are?
How much the world needs it. How easily it is done.
How instantaneously it acts. How infallibly it is
remembered. How superabundantly it pays itself back.

HENRY DRUMMOND

An instant of pure love is more precious to God...
than all other good works together,
though it may seem as if nothing were done.

JOHN OF THE CROSS

You who have received so much love share
it with others. Love others the way that
God has loved you, with tenderness.

MOTHER TERESA

When you put on a luncheon or a banquet...
invite the poor, the crippled, the lame, and the
blind. Then...God will reward you for inviting
those who could not repay you.

Luke 14:12–14 NLT

*In God's wisdom, He frequently
chooses to meet our needs by showing
His love toward us through
the hands and hearts of others.*

Jack Hayford

Personal Trainer

Do not follow foolish stories that disagree with God's truth, but train yourself to serve God. Training your body helps you in some ways, but serving God helps you in every way by bringing you blessings in this life and in the future life, too.... Command and teach these things. Do not let anyone treat you as if you are unimportant because you are young. Instead, be an example to the believers with your words, your actions, your love, your faith, and your pure life.

1 TIMOTHY 4:7–8, 11–12 NCV

Now may God himself, the God of peace, make you pure, belonging only to him. May your whole self–spirit, soul, and body–be kept safe and without fault when our Lord Jesus Christ comes. You can trust the One who calls you to do that for you.

1 THESSALONIANS 5:23–24 NCV

The LORD says, "I will guide you along the best pathway for your life. I will advise you and watch over you...." Unfailing love surrounds those who trust the LORD. So rejoice in the LORD and be glad!

PSALM 32:8, 10–11 NLT

God's training is for right now, not for some mist-shrouded future. His purpose is for this minute.... This moment is the future for which you've been preparing!

JONI EARECKSON TADA

Of One Heart

When two people love each other deeply and are
committed for life, they have usually developed a great
volume of understandings between them that would
be considered insignificant to anyone else. They share
countless private memories unknown to the rest of the
world. That is in large measure where their sense of
specialness to one another originates.

JAMES DOBSON

To love other people means to see them
as God intended them to be.

Oh, the miraculous energy that flows between two
people who care enough...to take the risks of...
responding with the whole heart.

ALEX NOBLE

Love creates a special world for two people. Everything
within it is guarded and preserved
by commitment, faithfulness, and trust.
Everything about it is enriched and endeared
by kindness, gentleness, and care.

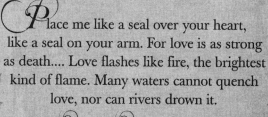

Place me like a seal over your heart, like a seal on your arm. For love is as strong as death.... Love flashes like fire, the brightest kind of flame. Many waters cannot quench love, nor can rivers drown it.

Song of Songs 8:6–7 NLT

*Love does not allow lovers
to belong anymore to themselves,
but they belong only to the Beloved.*

Dionysius

Unfailing Love

The LORD looks down from heaven and sees the
whole human race. From his throne he observes all
who live on the earth. He made their hearts, so he
understands everything they do.... But the LORD
watches over those who fear him, those who rely on
his unfailing love. He rescues them from death and
keeps them alive in times of famine.
We put our hope in the LORD. He is our help and our
shield. In him our hearts rejoice, for we trust in his
holy name. Let your unfailing love surround us, LORD,
for our hope is in you alone.

PSALM 33:13–15, 18–22 NLT

I know that He who is far outside the whole creation
takes me within Himself and hides me in His arms.

SYMEON

How we thank you, Lord! Your mighty
miracles give proof that you care.

PSALM 75:1 TLB

*Y*ou will trust God
only as much as you love Him.
And you will love Him not because
you have studied Him;
you will love Him because you have
touched Him—
in response to His touch.

BRENNAN MANNING

*Let the morning bring me word
of your unfailing love,
for I have put my trust in you.*

PSALM 143:8 NIV

The Best Thing

Love is not getting, but giving. Not a wild dream of pleasure and a madness of desire—oh, no—love is not that! It is goodness and honor and peace and pure living—yes, love is that and it is the best thing in the world and the thing that lives the longest.

HENRY VAN DYKE

To love and to be loved the wise would give...
All that for which alone the unwise live.

WALTER S. LANDOR

Love seeks one thing only: the good of the one loved. It leaves all the other secondary effects to take care of themselves. Love, therefore, is its own reward.

THOMAS MERTON

The LORD has told you...what is good; he has told you what he wants from you: to do what is right to other people, love being kind to others, and live humbly, obeying your God.

MICAH 6:8 NCV

GOD, our God! G OD the one and only!
Love G OD, your God, with your whole heart:
love him with all that's in you, love him with all
you've got! Write these commandments
that I've given you today on your hearts.
Get them inside of you.

DEUTERONOMY 6:4–6 THE MESSAGE

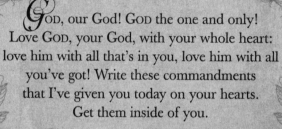

To love God, to serve Him
because we love Him, is...our
highest happiness.

HANNAH MORE

To See Anew

God looks at the world through the eyes of love.
If we, therefore, as human beings made in the
image of God also want to see reality rationally,
that is, as it truly is, then we, too, must learn
to look at what we see with love.

ROBERTA BONDI

Give us, Lord: a pure heart that we may see Thee,
a humble heart that we may hear Thee,
a heart of love that we may serve Thee,
a heart of faith that we may live Thee.

DAG HAMMARSKJÖLD

GOD, your God, will cut away the thick calluses on
your heart...freeing you to love GOD, your God, with
your whole heart and soul and live, really live.... And
you will make a new start, listening obediently to GOD,
keeping all his commandments.... Love GOD, your
God. Walk in his ways. Keep his commandments,
regulations, and rules so that you will live, really live,
live exuberantly, blessed by GOD.... Love GOD,
your God, listening obediently to him, firmly
embracing him. Oh yes, he is life itself.

DEUTERONOMY 30:6, 8, 16, 20 THE MESSAGE

*Y*et this I call to mind and therefore I have hope: Because of the LORD's great love we are not consumed, for his compassions never fail. They are new every morning; great is your faithfulness.

*L*AMENTATIONS 3:21–23 NIV

*L*ife begins each morning…. Each morning is the open door to a new world—new vistas, new aims, new tryings.

*L*EIGH *M*ITCHELL *H*ODGES

Response of the Heart

Love is the response of the heart to the overwhelming
goodness of God, so come in simply and speak to Him
in unvarnished honesty. You may be so awestruck and
full of love at His presence that words do not come.
This is all right!

RICHARD J. FOSTER

Fantastic changes can be made in feelings
with an honest heart-to-heart talk. For in
the presence of melted hearts wrongs are forgiven
and hurt hearts healed.

DORIS M. McDOWELL

The reflective life is a life that is attentive, receptive,
and responsive to what God is doing in us and around
us. It's a life that asks God to reach into our heart,
allowing Him to touch us there.

KEN GIRE

*H*ear me as I pray, O Lord.
Be merciful and answer me!
My heart has heard you say,
   "Come and talk with me."
And my heart responds,
   "Lord, I am coming."

*P*salm 27:7–8 nlt

*G*ratitude is the homage of the heart,
rendered to God for His goodness.
Nathaniel Parker Willis

What Really Matters

So this is my prayer: that your love will flourish and that you will not only love much but well. Learn to love appropriately. You need to use your head and test your feelings so that your love is sincere and intelligent, not sentimental gush.
Live a lover's life, circumspect and exemplary, a life Jesus will be proud of: bountiful in fruits from the soul, making Jesus Christ attractive to all, getting everyone involved in the glory and praise of God.

PHILIPPIANS 1:9–11 THE MESSAGE

Suppose someone has enough to live and sees a brother or sister in need, but does not help. Then God's love is not living in that person. My children, we should love people not only with words and talk, but by our actions and true caring. This is the way we know that we belong to the way of truth.

1 JOHN 3:17–19 NCV

Steep yourself in God-reality,
God-initiative, God-provisions.
You'll find all your everyday human
concerns will be met.
Don't be afraid of missing out.
You're my dearest friends!
The Father wants to give you the
very kingdom itself.

Luke 12:31–32 the message

Service is the rent we each pay for living.
It is not something to do in your spare time;
it is the very purpose of life.

Marian Wright Edelman

Inspiration to Love

Look deep within yourself and recognize what brings
life and grace into your heart. It is this that can be
shared with those around you. You are loved by God.
This is an inspiration to love.

CHRISTOPHER DE VINCK

Life is what we are alive to.
It is not length but breadth....
Be alive to...goodness, kindness, purity, love, history,
poetry, music, flowers, stars, God, and eternal hope.

MALTBIE D. BABCOCK

I love those who love me; and those who diligently
seek me will find me.

PROVERBS 8:17 NASB

If you are seeking after God, you may be sure of this:
God is seeking you much more. He is the Lover, and
you are His beloved. He has promised Himself to you.

JOHN OF THE CROSS

To know Him is to love Him and to know Him better is to love Him more.... As we go on to know Him better we shall find it a source of unspeakable joy that God is just what He is.

A.W. Tozer

The reason we can dare to risk loving others is that "God has for Christ's sake loved us." Think of it! We are loved eternally, totally, individually, unreservedly! Nothing can take God's love away.

Gloria Gaither

Surprise Us with Love

Surprise us with love at daybreak;
then we'll skip and dance all the day long....
Let your servants see what you're best at—
the ways you rule and bless your children.
And let the loveliness of our Lord, our God,
rest on us, confirming the work that we do.
Oh, yes. Affirm the work that we do!

PSALM 90:14, 16–17 THE MESSAGE

But me he caught—
reached all the way from sky to sea;
he pulled me out
of that ocean of hate, that enemy chaos,
the void in which I was drowning.
They hit me when I was down,
but GOD stuck by me.
He stood me up on a wide-open field;
I stood there saved—surprised to be loved!

PSALM 18:16–19 THE MESSAGE

*S*how the wonder of your great love, you who save by your right hand those who take refuge in you.... Keep me as the apple of your eye; hide me in the shadow of your wings.

*P*SALM 17:7–8 NIV

*I*nto all our lives, in many simple,
familiar...ways, God infuses
this element of joy from the surprises of life,
which unexpectedly brighten our days,
and fill our eyes with light.

*S*AMUEL *L*ONGFELLOW

His Touch

Those who draw near to God
One step through doubtings dim,
God will advance a mile
In blazing light to them.

The Lord's chief desire is to reveal Himself to you,
and in order for Him to do that, He gives you
abundant grace. The Lord gives you the experience
of enjoying His presence. He touches you,
and His touch is so delightful that, more than ever,
you are drawn inwardly to Him.

MADAME JEANNE GUYON

The sunshine dancing on the water, the lulling sound
of waves rolling into the shore, the glittering stars
against the night sky—all God's light, His warmth,
His majesty—our Father of light reaching out to us,
drawing each of us closer to Himself.

God loved us, and through his grace he gave us a good
hope and encouragement that continues forever.

2 THESSALONIANS 2:17 NCV

*I*n difficulites, I can drink freely of God's power and experience His touch of refreshment and blessing—much like an invigorating early spring rain.

ANABEL GILHAM

*G*od's Spirit touches our spirits and confirms who we really are. We know who he is, and we know who we are: Father and children.

ROMANS 8:16 THE MESSAGE

Joy is the touch of God's finger. The object of our longing is not the touch but the Toucher. This is true of all good things—they are all God's touch. Whatever we desire, we are really desiring God.

PETER KREEFT

Generous in Love

For GOD is sheer beauty, all-generous in love,
loyal always and ever.

PSALM 100:5 THE MESSAGE

Every path he guides us on is fragrant with
his loving-kindness and his truth.

PSALM 25:10 TLB

If you have any encouragement from being united with
Christ, if any comfort from his love...then make my joy
complete by being like-minded, having the same love,
being one in spirit and purpose.

PHILIPPIANS 2:1–2 NIV

The Creator thinks enough of you to have sent
Someone very special so that you might have life–
abundantly, joyfully, completely, and victoriously.

Real wisdom, God's wisdom, begins with a holy life and is characterized by getting along with others. It is gentle and reasonable, overflowing with mercy and blessings, not hot one day and cold the next, not two-faced. You can develop a healthy, robust community that lives right with God and enjoy its results only if you do the hard work of getting along with each other, treating each other with dignity and honor.

James 3:17–18 THE MESSAGE

Be happy with what you have and are, be generous with both, and you won't have to hunt for happiness.
William E. Gladstone

My Father's Child

Don't we all long for a father who, even though
our mistakes are written all over the wall,
will love us anyway? Don't we want a father
who cares for us in spite of our failures? We do
have that type of a father.... A father whose
grace is strongest when our devotion is weakest.

MAX LUCADO

If God, like a father, denies us what we want now,
it is in order to give us some far better thing
later on. The will of God, we can rest assured,
is invariably a better thing.

ELISABETH ELLIOT

God is a rich and bountiful Father, and He does not
forget His children, nor withhold from them anything
which it would be to their advantage to receive.

J. K. MACLEAN

Lift up your eyes. Your heavenly Father waits to bless you—in inconceivable ways to make your life what you never dreamed it could be.

ANNE ORTLUND

How great is the love the Father has lavished on us, that we should be called children of God! And that is what we are!

1 JOHN 3:1 NIV

When we call on God, He bends down His ear to listen, as a father bends down to listen to his little child.

ELIZABETH CHARLES

Tender Love

For all God's words are right, and everything he does
is worthy of our trust. He loves whatever is just and
good; the earth is filled with his tender love.

PSALM 33:4–5 TLB

Are you tired? Worn out? Burned out on religion?
Come to me. Get away with me and you'll recover
your life. I'll show you how to take a real rest. Walk
with me and work with me—watch how I do it.
Learn the unforced rhythms of grace. I won't lay
anything heavy or ill-fitting on you. Keep company
with me and you'll learn to live freely and lightly.

MATTHEW 11:28–30 THE MESSAGE

May the Lord direct your hearts into the
love of God.... May the Lord of peace
Himself continually grant you peace
in every circumstance.

2 THESSALONIANS 3:5, 16 NASB

$\mathcal{Y}$ou are tenderly and eternally loved
by the One who created you.

$\mathcal{H}$e is everything that is good and
comfortable for us. He is our clothing that
for love wraps us, clasps us,
and all surrounds us for tender love.

JULIAN OF NORWICH

Love Expressed

Affection is not much good unless it is expressed.
What's more, I have a notion that unexpressed
feelings have a tendency to shrink, wither, and
ultimately die. Putting an emotion into words gives
it a life and a reality that otherwise it doesn't have.

SIR ARTHUR GORDON

Those who are steadily learning how to love are
enabled to do this because the very love of God
Himself has been put into our hearts. We do
not have to whip up feelings of affection or
emotion which we might recognize as love.
Love is already there if Christ is there.

EUGENIA PRICE

Some emotions don't make a lot of noise.
It's hard to hear pride.
Caring is real faint—like a heartbeat.
And pure love—why, some days it's so quiet,
You don't even know it's there.

ERMA BOMBECK

*A*nd God raised us up with Christ and seated us with him in the heavenly realms in Christ Jesus, in order that in the coming ages he might show the incomparable riches of his grace, expressed in his kindness to us in Christ Jesus. For it is by grace you have been saved, through faith—and this not from yourselves, it is the gift of God.

*E*PHESIANS 2:6–8 NIV

*A*ll that we have and are is one of the unique and never-to-be repeated ways God has chosen to express Himself in space and time.

*B*RENNAN *M*ANNING

God's Lovingkindness

The LORD is my light and my salvation—whom shall I
fear? The LORD is the stronghold of my life—of whom
shall I be afraid?... One thing I ask of the LORD,
this is what I seek: that I may dwell in the house of
the LORD all the days of my life, to gaze upon
the beauty of the LORD and to seek him in his temple.
For in the day of trouble he will keep me
safe in his dwelling; he will hide me in the shelter of
his tabernacle and set me high upon a rock.... I am still
confident of this: I will see the goodness of the LORD
in the land of the living. Wait for the LORD;
be strong and take heart and wait for the LORD.

PSALM 27:1, 4–5, 13–14 NIV

For Your lovingkindness is before my eyes,
and I have walked in Your truth.

PSALM 26:3 NASB

Not to us, O LORD, not to us, but to Your name give glory because of Your lovingkindness, because of Your truth.

PSALM 115:1 NASB

Let him that glorieth glory in this, that he understandeth and knoweth me, that I am the LORD which exercise lovingkindness, judgment, and righteousness, in the earth: for in these things I delight.

JEREMIAH 9:24 KJV

We may...depend upon God's promises, for...He will be as good as His word. He is so kind that He cannot deceive us, so true that He cannot break His promise.

MATTHEW HENRY

Intimacy with God

Our joy will be complete if we remain in
His love—for His love is personal, intimate,
real, living, delicate, faithful love.

MOTHER TERESA

God reads the secrets of the heart.
God reads its most intimate feelings,
even those which we are not aware of.

JEAN-NICHOLAS GROU

It's usually through our hard times, the unexpected
and not-according-to-plan times, that we
experience God in more intimate ways. We
discover an unquenchable longing to know
Him more. It's a passion that isn't concerned
that life fall within certain predictable lines,
but a passion that pursues God and knows He is
relentless in His pursuit of each one of us.

WENDY MOORE

There are times when I draw near
enough to touch Him. Then I know that
He has been there all the time.

GLORIA GAITHER

Come close to God,
and God will come close to you....
Humble yourselves before the Lord,
and he will lift you up in honor.

JAMES 4:8, 10 NLT

That is God's call to us—simply to be
people who are content to live close to Him
and to renew the kind of life in which
the closeness is felt and experienced.

THOMAS MERTON

At Home in His Love

Make your home in me just as I do in you.
In the same way that a branch can't bear grapes by
itself but only by being joined to the vine, you can't
bear fruit unless you are joined with me.
I am the Vine, you are the branches. When you're
joined with me and I with you, the relation intimate
and organic, the harvest is sure to be abundant.
Separated, you can't produce a thing....
But if you make yourselves at home with me and
my words are at home in you, you can be sure that
whatever you ask will be listened to and acted upon....
I've loved you the way my Father has loved me.
Make yourselves at home in my love.

JOHN 15:4–5, 7, 9 THE MESSAGE

This is and has been the Father's work from the
beginning—to bring us into the home of His heart.

GEORGE MACDONALD

*H*ow lovely are Your dwelling places, O LORD of hosts! My soul longed and even yearned for the courts of the LORD; my heart and my flesh sing for joy to the living God.... For a day in Your courts is better than a thousand outside.

*P*SALM 84:1–2, 10 NASB

*M*y life is merely a whisper of the breath of God, but it is His breath, His grace, His life in me.

*P*HIL *J*OEL

No Matter What

Get a pure heart from God and you can be supremely
happy no matter what the circumstances and no matter
what is going on around you.

BILLY GRAHAM

The abundant life that Jesus talked about begins
with the unfathomable Good News put simply:
My dear child, I love you anyway.

ALICE CHAPIN

Nothing we can do will make the Father love us less;
nothing we do can make Him love us more.
He loves us unconditionally with an everlasting love.
All He asks of us is that we respond to Him with
the free will that He has given to us.

NANCIE CARMICHAEL

No matter what our past may have held,
and no matter how many future days we have,
God stands beside us and loves us.

GARY SMALLEY AND JOHN TRENT

"Though the mountains be shaken and the hills be removed, yet my unfailing love for you will not be shaken nor my covenant of peace be removed," says the LORD, who has compassion on you.

ISAIAH 54:10 NIV

God's forgiveness and love exist for you as if you were the only person on earth.

CECIL OSBORNE

Trust in His Love

Look at the birds of the air, that they do not sow, nor reap nor gather into barns, and yet your heavenly Father feeds them. Are you not worth much more than they? And who of you by being worried can add a single hour to his life? And why are you worried about clothing? Observe how the lilies of the field grow; they do not toil nor do they spin, yet I say to you that not even Solomon in all his glory clothed himself like one of these. But if God so clothes the grass of the field, which is alive today and tomorrow is thrown into the furnace, will He not much more clothe you? You of little faith! Do not worry then, saying, "What will we eat?" or "What will we drink?" or "What will we wear for clothing?" For...your heavenly Father knows that you need all these things. But seek first His kingdom and His righteousness, and all these things will be added to you.

MATTHEW 6:26–33 NASB

If you believe in God, it is not too difficult to believe that He is concerned about the universe and all the events on this earth. But the really staggering message of the Bible is that this same God cares deeply about you and your identity and the events of your life.... We have missed the full impact of the gospel if we have not discovered what it is to be ourselves, loved by God, irreplaceable in His sight, unique among our fellow men.

BRUCE LARSON

Trust the past to the mercy of God, the present to His love, and the future to His Providence.

AUGUSTINE

God Knows Me

What matters supremely is not the fact that I know
God, but the larger fact which underlies it—the fact that
He knows me. I am graven on the palms of His hands.
I am never out of His mind.
All my knowledge of Him depends on His sustained
initiative in knowing me. I know Him because
He first knew me and continues to know me.

J. I. PACKER

In those times I can't seem to find God, I rest
in the assurance that He knows how to find me.

NEVA COYLE

Dear friends, we should love each other,
because love comes from God. Everyone who
loves has become God's child and knows God.
Whoever does not love does not know God,
because God is love.

1 JOHN 4:7–8 NCV

God knows the rhythm of my spirit and knows
my heart thoughts. He is as close as breathing.

From the heart of God comes the strongest rhythm–the rhythm of love. Without His love reverberating in us, whatever we do will come across like a noisy gong or a clanging symbol. And so the work of the human heart, it seems to me, is to listen for that music and pick up on its rhythms.

Ken Gire

Nevertheless, God's solid foundation stands firm, sealed with this inscription: "The Lord knows those who are his."

2 Timothy 2:19 NIV

Rest in His Love

I want you woven into a tapestry of love,
in touch with everything there is to know
of God. Then you will have minds confident
and at rest, focused on Christ, God's great mystery.
All the richest treasures of wisdom and knowledge
are embedded in that mystery and nowhere else.
And we've been shown the mystery!

COLOSSIANS 2:2–3 THE MESSAGE

Let the beloved of the LORD rest secure in him,
for he shields him all day long, and the one the
LORD loves rests between his shoulders.

DEUTERONOMY 33:12 NIV

Relax, everything's going to be all right; rest,
everything's coming together; open your hearts,
love is on the way!

JUDE 1:2 THE MESSAGE

*F*aith is a letting go,
an abandonment, an abiding rest
in God that nothing can disturb.

*T*he LORD will guide you always; he will
satisfy your needs in a sun-scorched land....
You will be like a well-watered garden,
like a spring whose waters never fail.

*I*SAIAH 58:11 NIV

*T*he crashing wave finally reaches peace
as it breaks upon the land...so our
turbulent spirits find rest, as we break
upon the vast shoreline of God's love.

*J*ANET *L. W*EAVER *S*MITH

Really Live

Now comfort me so I can live, really live;
your revelation is the tune I dance to.

PSALM 119:77 THE MESSAGE

I'm feeling terrible—I couldn't feel worse! Get me
on my feet again. You promised, remember?
When I told my story, you responded; train me
well in your deep wisdom. Help me understand
these things inside and out so I can ponder your
miracle-wonders. My sad life's dilapidated,
a falling-down barn; build me up again by
your Word. Barricade the road that goes Nowhere;
grace me with your clear revelation. I choose the true
road to Somewhere, I post your road signs at every
curve and corner. I grasp and cling to whatever you
tell me; GOD, don't let me down! I'll run the course
you lay out for me if you'll just show me how.

PSALM 119:25 THE MESSAGE

I asked God for all things that I might enjoy life.
He gave me life that I might enjoy all things.

When someone gives you a hard time,
respond with the energies of prayer,
for then you are working out of your true
selves, your God-created selves.... Live out
your God-created identity. Live generously
and graciously toward others,
the way God lives toward you.

MATTHEW 5:44–45, 48 THE MESSAGE

Let God have you, and let God love you—
and don't be surprised if your heart begins
to hear music you've never heard and your
feet learn to dance as never before.

MAX LUCADO

Genuine Heart-Hunger

Genuine heart-hunger, accompanied by sincere seeking
after eternal values, does not go unrewarded.

JUSTINE KNIGHT

The heart is rich when it is content, and it
is always content when its desires are fixed
on God. Nothing can bring greater happiness
than doing God's will for the love of God.

MIGUEL FEBRES CORDERO-MUÑOZ

The overflowing life does not just happen.
It is only as our own deep thirst is quenched, only
as we are filled ourselves, that we can be channels
through which His overflow reaches other lives.

GRACE STRICKER DAWSON

Come and sit and ask Him whatever is on
your heart. No question is too small, no riddle
too simple. He has all the time in the world.

MAX LUCADO

*G*od's pantry never runs low.
His wells never run dry.

*C*HARLES *R*. *S*WINDOLL

*B*lessed are those who hunger and thirst for
righteousness, for they shall be satisfied.

*M*ATTHEW 5:6 NASB

*T*he place where God calls you to is
*the place where your deep gladness
and the world's deep hunger meet.*

*F*REDERICK *B*UECHNER

Live in Harmony

Finally, all of you, live in harmony with one another;
be sympathetic, love..., be compassionate and humble.
Do not repay evil with evil or insult with insult, but
with blessing, because to this you were called so that
you may inherit a blessing.

1 PETER 3:8–9 NIV

Love comes while we rest against our
Father's chest. Joy comes when we catch the
rhythms of His heart. Peace comes when we
live in harmony with those rhythms.

KEN GIRE

Peace is not placidity: peace is the power to endure the
megatron of pain with joy, the silent thunder of release,
the ordering of Love. Peace is the atom's start, the
primal image: God within the heart.

MADELEINE L'ENGLE

God cannot give us a happiness and peace apart from Himself, because it is not there. There is no such thing.

C. S. Lewis

When people's lives please the LORD, even their enemies are at peace with them.

Proverbs 16:7 NLT

God's peace is joy resting.
His joy is peace dancing.

F. F. Bruce

Love without Limits

Before anything else, above all else, beyond everything
else, God loves us. God loves us extravagantly,
ridiculously, without limit or condition.
God is in love with us...God yearns for us.

ROBERTA BONDI

There is no limit to God's love. It is without measure
and its depth cannot be sounded.

MOTHER TERESA

With God our trust can be abandoned, utterly free.
In Him are no limitations, no flaws, no weaknesses.
His judgment is perfect, His knowledge of us is perfect,
His love is perfect. God alone is trustworthy.
EUGENIA PRICE

Everything which relates to God is infinite. We must
therefore, while we keep our hearts humble, keep our
aims high. Our highest services are indeed but finite,
imperfect. But as God is unlimited in goodness,
He should have our unlimited love.

HANNAH MORE

*G*od already loves us as much as an
infinite God can possibly love.

PHILIP YANCEY

I lavish unfailing love for a thousand
generations on those who love me
and obey my commands.

EXODUS 20:6 NLT

*G*od loves us for ourselves. He values
our love more than He values galaxies
of new created worlds.

A. W. TOZER

The Love of God

Can anything ever separate us from Christ's love?
Does it mean he no longer loves us if we have trouble
or calamity, or are persecuted, or hungry, or destitute,
or in danger, or threatened with death?... No, despite
all these things, overwhelming victory is ours
through Christ, who loved us.
And I am convinced that nothing can ever separate
us from God's love. Neither death nor life, neither
angels nor demons, neither our fears for today nor
our worries about tomorrow—not even the powers of
hell can separate us from God's love. No power in the
sky above or in the earth below—indeed, nothing in all
creation will ever be able to separate us from the love
of God that is revealed in Christ Jesus our Lord.

ROMANS 8:35, 37–39 NLT

Nothing can separate you from His love,
absolutely nothing.... God is enough for time,
and God is enough for eternity. God is enough!

HANNAH WHITALL SMITH

*W*e also have joy with our troubles,
because we know that these troubles
produce patience. And patience produces
character, and character produces hope.
And this hope will never disappoint us, because
God has poured out his love to fill
our hearts. He gave us his love through the
Holy Spirit, whom God has given to us.

ROMANS 5:3–5 NCV

*To be grateful is to recognize the
love of God in everything He has
given us—and He has given us everything.
Every breath we draw is a gift of His love,
every moment of existence is a gift of grace.*

THOMAS MERTON

The Meaning of Friendship

By friendship you mean the greatest love,
the greatest usefulness, the most open communication,
the noblest sufferings,
the severest counsel, the greatest union of minds
of which brave men and women are capable.

JEREMY TAYLOR

Whoever loves pure thoughts and kind
words will have even the king as a friend.

PROVERBS 22:11 NCV

Friends are an indispensable part of a meaningful life.
They are the ones who share our burdens
and multiply our blessings. A true friend sticks
by us in our joys and sorrows. In good times
and bad, we need friends who will pray for us,
listen to us, and lend a comforting hand and an
understanding ear when needed.
BEVERLY LAHAYE

A good friend will sharpen your character,
draw your soul into the light, and challenge
your heart to love in a greater way.

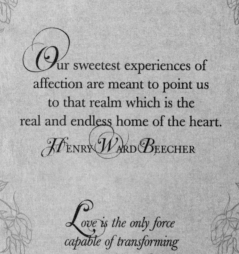

*O*ur sweetest experiences of
affection are meant to point us
to that realm which is the
real and endless home of the heart.

*H*ENRY *W*ARD *B*EECHER

*L*ove is the only force
capable of transforming
an enemy into a friend.

*M*ARTIN *L*UTHER *K*ING *J*R.

How He Loves Us!

Blue skies with white clouds on summer days.
A myriad of stars on clear moonlit nights.
Tulips and roses and violets and dandelions and daisies.
Bluebirds and laughter and sunshine and Easter.
See how He loves us!

ALICE CHAPIN

Our Creator would never have made such lovely
days, and have given us the deep hearts to enjoy them,
above and beyond all thought, unless we were meant
to be immortal.

NATHANIEL HAWTHORNE

His tenderness in the springing grass,
His beauty in the flowers,
His living love in the sun above—
All here, and near, and ours.

CHARLOTTE PERKINS GILMAN

*H*e paints the lily of the field,
Perfumes each lily bell;
If He so loves the little flowers,
I know He loves me well.

MARIA STRAUS

*M*ay they who love you be like
the sun when it rises in its strength.

JUDGES 5:31 NIV

O God, *creator of light:*
at the rising of Your sun this morning,
let the greatest of all lights,
Your love, rise like the sun
within our hearts.

True Living Devotion

Regardless of whether we feel strong or weak in our faith, we remember that our assurance is not based upon our ability to conjure up some special feeling. Rather, it is built upon a confident assurance in the faithfulness of God. We focus on His trustworthiness and especially on His steadfast love.

RICHARD J. FOSTER

When faithfulness is most difficult, it can be most rewarding. True living presupposes the love of God; indeed, it is itself a true love of Him in the highest form. Divine love, enlightening our soul and making us pleasing to God, is called grace. Giving us power to do good, it is called charity. When it reaches the point of perfection where it makes us earnestly, frequently, and readily do good, it is called devotion.

FRANCIS DE SALES

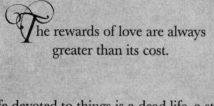

The rewards of love are always
greater than its cost.

A life devoted to things is a dead life, a stump;
a God-shaped life is a flourishing tree.

PROVERBS 11:28 THE MESSAGE

*It is love that asks, that seeks,
that knocks, that finds,
and that is faithful to what it finds.*

AUGUSTINE

The Roots of Love

I pray that from his glorious, unlimited resources
he will empower you with inner strength through
his Spirit. Then Christ will make his home in your
hearts as you trust in him. Your roots will grow
down into God's love and keep you strong. And
may you have the power to understand, as all God's
people should, how wide, how long, how high, and
how deep his love is. May you experience the love
of Christ, though it is too great to understand fully.
Then you will be made complete with all the fullness
of life and power that comes from God. Now all
glory to God, who is able, through his mighty power
at work within us, to accomplish infinitely more than
we might ask or think.

EPHESIANS 3:16–20 NLT

The love of God is broader
than the measure of our mind
And the heart of the Eternal
is most wonderfully kind.

FREDERICK W. FABER

May you be ever present
in the garden of His love.

If the part of the dough offered as
firstfruits is holy, then the whole batch is holy;
if the root is holy, so are the branches.

ROMANS 11:16 NIV

*A wise gardener plants his seeds,
then has the good sense not to dig them up
every few days to see if a crop is on the way.
Likewise, we must be patient as God brings
the answers...in His own good time.*

QUIN SHERRER

Desires of Your Heart

May God give you eyes to see beauty
only the heart can understand.

From the world we see, hear, and touch,
we behold inspired visions that reveal God's glory.
In the sun's light, we catch warm rays of grace
and glimpse His eternal design. In the birds' song,
we hear His voice and it reawakens our desire
for Him. At the wind's touch, we feel His Spirit
and sense our eternal existence.

WENDY MOORE

In the central place of every heart, there is a recording
chamber; so long as it receives messages of beauty,
hope, cheer, and courage, so long you are young.

DOUGLAS MACARTHUR

May he give you the desire of your heart
and make all your plans succeed.

Psalm 20:4 NIV

He made you so you could share in His
creation, could love and laugh and know Him.

Ted Griffen

All the world is an utterance of the Almighty.
Its countless beauties, its exquisite adaptations,
all speak to you of Him.

Phillips Brooks

At All Times

I look up to the hills,
but where does my help come from?
My help comes from the LORD,
who made heaven and earth.
He will not let you be defeated.
He who guards you never sleeps.
He who guards Israel
never rests or sleeps.
The LORD guards you.
The LORD is the shade that
protects you from the sun.
The sun cannot hurt you during the day,
and the moon cannot hurt you at night.
The LORD will protect you from all dangers;
he will guard your life.
The LORD will guard you as you come and go,
both now and forever.

PSALM 121:1–8 NCV

The "air" which our souls need also envelops all of us at all times and on all sides. God is round about us...with many-sided and all-sufficient grace. All we need to do is to open our hearts.

Ole Hallesby

Be joyful always; pray continually; give thanks in all circumstances, for this is God's will for you in Christ Jesus.

1 Thessalonians 5:16–18 NIV

We have a Father in heaven who is almighty, who loves His children as He loves His only-begotten Son, and whose very joy and delight it is to...help them at all times and under all circumstances.

George Mueller

The Goodness of God

The goodness of God is infinitely more wonderful than we will ever be able to comprehend.

A.W. TOZER

All that is good, all that is true, all that is beautiful...be it great or small, be it perfect or fragmentary, natural as well as supernatural, moral as well as material, comes from God.

JOHN HENRY NEWMAN

We walk without fear, full of hope and courage and strength to do His will, waiting for the endless good which He is always giving as fast as He can get us able to take it in.

GEORGE MACDONALD

Savor little glimpses of God's goodness and His majesty, thankful for the gift of them: winding pathways through the woods, a bright green canopy overhead, and dappled sunshine falling all around, warm upon our faces.

*O*pen your mouth and taste, open your eyes and see—how good GOD is. Blessed are you who run to him. Worship GOD if you want the best; worship opens doors to all his goodness.

*P*SALM 34:8–9 THE MESSAGE

In extravagance of soul
we seek His face.
In generosity of heart,
we glean His gentle touch.
In excessiveness of spirit,
we love Him and His love
comes back to us a hundredfold.

*T*RICIA *M*C*C*ARY *R*HODES

Forever Love

The LORD is like a father to his children, tender
and compassionate to those who fear him. For he
understands how weak we are; he knows we are only
dust. Our days on earth are like grass; like wildflowers,
we bloom and die. The wind blows,
and we are gone—as though we had never been here.
But the love of the LORD remains forever.

PSALM 103:13–17 NLT

The LORD is gracious and compassionate, slow to
anger and rich in love. The LORD is good to all; he has
compassion on all he has made.... The LORD is faithful
to all his promises and loving toward all he has made.

PSALM 145:8–9, 13 NIV

Let them give thanks to the LORD
for his unfailing love.

PSALM 107:8 NIV

*P*raise the LORD, all you nations;
extol him, all you peoples.
For great is his love toward us,
and the faithfulness of the LORD
endures forever.
Praise the LORD.

*P*SALM 117:1–2 NIV

*H*erein is joy, amid the ebb and flow
of the passing world:
our God remains unmoved,
and His throne endures forever.

*R*OBERT *E*. *C*OLEMAN

True Love

Love isn't the tingly sensation you feel when you
hold someone's hand for the first time. Love isn't
the breath-catching feeling you have when you
know someone thinks only of you.
True, lasting love comes after struggling together
through the hard times, remembering the good
times, and having faith that God will help you over
one more hill together.
True love is accepting yourself with all
your strengths and weaknesses and accepting
the other person in the same way.

RHONDA S. HOGAN

Romance is flattering attention.
Love is genuine thoughtfulness....
Romance is tingling excitement.
Love is tenderness, constancy, being cherished.

MARJORIE HOLMES

True love risks itself—risks not being loved—
for the ultimate good of the loved one.

GLORIA GAITHER

And now these three remain:
faith, hope and love.
But the greatest of these is love.

1 CORINTHIANS 13:13 NIV

Love, you know,
Seeks to make happy
Rather than to be happy.

RALPH CONNOR

Pour Out Your Heart

I find rest in God;
only he can save me.
He is my rock and my salvation.
He is my defender;
I will not be defeated....
I find rest in God;
only he gives me hope....
My honor and salvation come from God.
He is my mighty rock and my protection.

PSALM 62:1–2, 5, 7 NCV

Trust in him at all times, O people; pour out your
hearts to him, for God is our refuge.... One thing God
has spoken, two things have I heard: that you, O God,
are strong, and that you, O Lord, are loving.

PSALM 62:8, 11–12 NIV

The LORD will work out his plans
for my life—for your faithful love,
O LORD, endures forever.

PSALM 138:8 NLT

Rest in the LORD and wait patiently for Him.

PSALM 37:7 NASB

When God finds a soul that rests in Him
and is not easily moved...to this same soul
He gives the joy of His presence.

CATHERINE OF GENOA

Love in the Real World

True love is but a humble, lowborn thing....
It is a thing to walk with hand in hand, through
the everydayness of this workaday world.

JAMES RUSSELL LOWELL

When true love comes, that which is counterfeit
will be recognized. For someday it will rain on the
picnic, ants will sting, mosquitoes will bite, and you
will get indigestion from the potato salad. There
will be no stars in your eyes, no sunsets on your
horizon. Love will be in black and white with no
piped-in music. But you will say "forever," because
love is a choice you have made.

RUTH SENTER

Always be humble and gentle. Be patient
with each other, making allowance for each
other's faults because of your love.

EPHESIANS 4:2 NLT

*B*e content with who you are, and don't put on airs. God's strong hand is on you; he'll promote you at the right time. Live carefree before God; he is most careful with you.

1 PETER 5:6–7 THE MESSAGE

I think true love is never blind
But rather brings an added light,
An inner vision quick to find
The beauties hid from common sight.

PHOEBE CARY

An Undivided Heart

Above all else, guard your heart,
for it is the wellspring of life.

PROVERBS 4:23 NIV

I will give them an undivided heart and put a new
spirit in them; I will remove from them their heart of
stone and give them a heart of flesh. Then...they will
be my people, and I will be their God.

EZEKIEL 11:19–20 NIV

"Which command in God's Law
is the most important?"
Jesus said, " 'Love the Lord your God with
all your passion and prayer and intelligence.'
This is the most important, the first on any list.
But there is a second to set alongside it:
'Love others as well as you love yourself.'
These two commands are pegs; everything in
God's Law and the Prophets hangs from them."

MATTHEW 22:36–40 THE MESSAGE

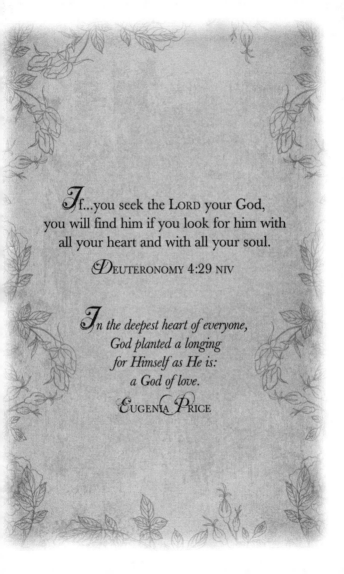

*I*f...you seek the LORD your God,
you will find him if you look for him with
all your heart and with all your soul.

*D*EUTERONOMY 4:29 NIV

*I*n the deepest heart of everyone,
God planted a longing
for Himself as He is:
a God of love.

*E*UGENIA *P*RICE

Share the Love

Love makes burdens lighter, because you divide them.
It makes joys more intense, because you share them.
It makes you stronger, so that you can reach
out and become involved with life in ways you
dared not risk alone.

Open your hearts to the love God instills....
God loves you tenderly. What He gives you is not
to be kept under lock and key, but to be shared.

MOTHER TERESA

Lord...give me the gift of faith to be renewed and
shared with others each day. Teach me to live this
moment only, looking neither to the past with regret,
nor the future with apprehension. Let love be my aim
and my life a prayer.

ROSEANN ALEXANDER-ISHAM

J give you a new command:
Love each other.
You must love each other
as I have loved you.

JOHN 13:34 NCV

The impetus of God's love
comes from within Himself,
to share with us His life and love.
It is a beautiful, eternal gift,
held out to us in the hands of love.
All we have to do is say "Yes!"

JOHN POWELL

My Cup Overflows

The LORD is my shepherd;
I have all that I need.
He lets me rest in green meadows;
he leads me beside peaceful streams.
He renews my strength.
He guides me along right paths,
bringing honor to his name.
Even when I walk through the darkest valley,
I will not be afraid,
for you are close beside me.
Your rod and your staff
protect and comfort me.
You prepare a feast for me
in the presence of my enemies.
You honor me by anointing my head with oil.
My cup overflows with blessings.
Surely your goodness and unfailing love will pursue me
all the days of my life,
and I will live in the house of the LORD forever.

PSALM 23:1–6 NLT

*Y*our thoughts—how rare, how beautiful!
God, I'll never comprehend them!
I couldn't even begin to count them—
any more than I could count
the sand of the sea.

*P*SALM 139:17 THE MESSAGE

*G*od never abandons anyone
on whom He has set His love;
nor does Christ, the good shepherd,
ever lose track of His sheep.

*J. I. P*ACKER

Made for Joy

Our hearts were made for joy. Our hearts were
made to enjoy the One who created them.
Too deeply planted to be much affected by
the ups and downs of life, this joy is a knowing
and a being known by our Creator.
He sets our hearts alight with radiant joy.

WENDY MOORE

Live for today but hold your hands open to tomorrow.
Anticipate the future and its changes with joy.
There is a seed of God's love in every event,
every circumstance...in which you may find yourself.

BARBARA JOHNSON

If one is joyful, it means that one is faithfully
living for God, and that nothing else counts; and if one
gives joy to others one is doing God's work.
With joy without and joy within, all is well.

JANET ERSKINE STUART

If nothing seems to go my
way today, this is my happiness:
God is my Father and I am His child.

BASILEA SCHLINK

Oh, the joys of those who...delight in the law
of the LORD, meditating on it day and night.
They are like trees planted along the
riverbank, bearing fruit each season
without fail. Their leaves never wither,
and they prosper in all they do.

PSALM 1:1–3 NLT

*God's friendship is
the unexpected joy we find
when we reach His outstretched hand.*

JANET L. WEAVER SMITH

Blessed by Love

God loves to look at us and loves it when we will look back at Him. Even when we try to run away from our troubles...God will find us, bless us, even when we feel most alone, unsure.... God will find a way to let us know that He is with us in this place, wherever we are.

KATHLEEN NORRIS

Bless the LORD, O my soul,
And all that is within me, bless His holy name.
Bless the LORD, O my soul,
And forget none of His benefits;
Who pardons all your iniquities,
Who heals all your diseases;
Who redeems your life from the pit,
Who crowns you with lovingkindness and compassion;
Who satisfies your years with good things,
So that your youth is renewed like the eagle.

PSALM 103:1–5 NASB

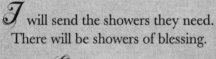

I will send the showers they need.
There will be showers of blessing.

*E*ZEKIEL 34:26 NLT

*B*e on the lookout for mercies.
The more we look for them,
the more of them we will see.
Blessings brighten
when we count them.

*M*ALTBIE *D.* *B*ABCOCK

Held in His Hand

The mystery of life is that the Lord of life cannot
be known except in and through the act of living.
Without the concrete and specific involvements of
daily life we cannot come to know the loving
presence of Him who holds us in the palm of
His hand.... Therefore, we are called each day to
present to our Lord the whole of our lives.

HENRI J. M. NOUWEN

God promises to keep us in the palm
of His hand, with or without our awareness.
God has already made a space for us,
even if we have not made a space for God.

DAVID AND BARBARA SORENSEN

The God who holds the whole world in His
hands wraps Himself in the splendor
of the sun's light and walks among the clouds.

That Hand which bears all nature up
shall guard His children well.

WILLIAM COWPER

Behold, I have inscribed you
on the palms of My hands.

ISAIAH 49:16 NASB

Listening to God is a firsthand experience....
God invites you to vacation in His splendor.
He invites you to feel the touch of His hand.
He invites you to feast at His table.
He wants to spend time with you.

MAX LUCADO

Love Never Fails

The LORD is compassionate and merciful,
slow to get angry and filled with unfailing love.
He will not constantly accuse us,
nor remain angry forever.
He does not punish us for all our sins;
he does not deal harshly with us, as we deserve.
For his unfailing love toward those who fear him
is as great as the height of the heavens above the earth.
He has removed our sins as far from us
as the east is from the west.

PSALM 103:8–12 NLT

This I call to mind and therefore I have hope:
Because of the LORD's great love
we are not consumed,
for his compassions never fail.
They are new every morning;
great is your faithfulness.

LAMENTATIONS 3:21–23 NIV

Show us your unfailing love, O Lord,
and grant us your salvation.

Psalm 85:7 niv

[God's] heart is the most
sensitive and tender of all.
No act goes unnoticed,
no matter how insignificant or small.

Richard J. Foster

Divine Romance

God's holy beauty comes near you, like a spiritual
scent, and it stirs your drowsing soul.... He creates
in you the desire to find Him and run after
Him—to follow wherever He leads you, and to press
peacefully against His heart wherever He is.

JOHN OF THE CROSS

To fall in love with God is the greatest of all romances—
to seek Him the greatest of all adventures,
to find Him the greatest human achievement.

AUGUSTINE

The light of God surrounds me,
The love of God enfolds me,
The presence of God watches over me,
Wherever I am, God is.

In the morning let our hearts gaze upon
God's love...and in the beauty of that vision,
let us go forth to meet the day.

ROY LESSIN

The greatest honor we can give God
is to live gladly because of the
knowledge of His love.

JULIAN OF NORWICH

You have made known to me the
path of life; you will fill me with
joy in your presence, with eternal
pleasures at your right hand.

PSALM 16:11 NIV

*The love of the Father is like a sudden rain shower
that will pour forth when you least expect it, catching
you up into wonder and praise.*

RICHARD J. FOSTER

Loved for Ourselves

Even before he made the world, God loved us and
chose us in Christ to be holy and without fault in
his eyes. God decided in advance to adopt us into
his own family by bringing us to himself through
Jesus Christ. This is what he wanted to do, and it
gave him great pleasure. So we praise God for the
glorious grace he has poured out on us who belong
to his dear Son. He is so rich in kindness and grace
that he purchased our freedom with the blood of
his Son and forgave our sins.
He has showered his kindness on us,
along with all wisdom and understanding.

EPHESIANS 1:4–8 NLT

The God who created, names, and numbers
the stars in the heavens also numbers the hairs
of my head.... He pays attention to very
big things and to very small ones.
What matters to me matters to Him,
and that changes my life.

ELISABETH ELLIOT

*G*od's love is meteoric,
his loyalty astronomic,
His purpose titanic,
his verdicts oceanic.
Yet in his largeness
nothing gets lost.

*P*SALM 36:5–6 THE MESSAGE

*G*od loves us for ourselves.
He values our love more than He values
galaxies of new created worlds.

*A.W.*TOZER

Promise of Love

Each time a rainbow appears, stretching from one end
of the sky to the other, it's God renewing His promise.
Each shade of color, each facet of light displays the
radiant spectrum of God's love—a promise that life can
be new for each one of us.

God's love never ceases. Never....
God doesn't love us less if we fail or more if we
succeed. God's love never ceases.

Max Lucado

God has not promised sun without rain,
joy without sorrow, peace without pain.
But God has promised strength for the day,
rest for the labor, light for the way,
grace for the trials, help from above,
unfailing sympathy, undying love.

Annie Johnson Flint

*G*od makes a promise—
faith believes it,
hope anticipates it,
patience quietly awaits it.

*O*nce again you will have compassion
on us.... You will show us your faithfulness
and unfailing love as you promised.

*M*ICAH 7:19–20 NLT

*I*t's only a tiny rosebud—
A flower of God's design;
But I cannot unfold the petals
With these clumsy hands of mine.
And the pathway that lies before me
Only my heavenly Father knows—
I'll trust Him to unfold the moments
Just as He unfolds the rose.

A Sense of Wholeness

Don't fret or worry. Instead of worrying, pray.
Let petitions and praises shape your worries
into prayers, letting God know your concerns.
Before you know it, a sense of God's wholeness,
everything coming together for good,
will come and settle you down. It's wonderful
what happens when Christ displaces worry
at the center of your life.

PHILIPPIANS 4:6–7 THE MESSAGE

There are two days in the week about which
I never worry. Two carefree days, kept sacredly free
from fear and apprehension. One of these days is
yesterday—and the other is tomorrow.

ROBERT BURDETTE

And now...one final thing. Fix your thoughts
on what is true, and honorable, and right, and pure,
and lovely, and admirable. Think about things that
are excellent and worthy of praise.

PHILIPPIANS 4:8 NLT

You'll go out in joy,
you'll be led into a whole and complete life.
The mountains and hills will lead the parade,
bursting with song. All the trees
of the forest will join the procession,
exuberant with applause.

*I*SAIAH 55:12 THE MESSAGE

*God did not tell us to follow Him
because He needed our help,
but because He knew that
loving Him would make us whole.*

*I*RENAEUS

Settled in Solitude

Solitude liberates us from entanglements by carving out a space from which we can see ourselves and our situation before the Audience of One. Solitude provides the private place where we can take our bearings and so make God our North Star.

Os Guinness

So wait before the Lord. Wait in the stillness. And in that stillness, assurance will come to you. You will know that you are heard; you will know that your Lord ponders the voice of your humble desires; you will hear quiet words spoken to you yourself, perhaps to your grateful surprise and refreshment.

Amy Carmichael

Whoever drinks the water I give will never be thirsty. The water I give will become a spring of water gushing up inside that person, giving eternal life.

John 4:13–14 NCV

"*Be still, and know that I am God;*
I will be exalted among the nations,
I will be exalted in the earth."

*P*SALM 46:10 NIV

*We must drink deeply from the
very Source the deep calm and peace
of interior quietude and refreshment of God,
allowing the pure water of
divine grace to flow plentifully
and unceasingly from the Source itself.*

*M*OTHER *T*ERESA

Practice Real Love

My dear children, let's not just talk about love;
let's practice real love. This is the only way we'll
know we're living truly, living in God's reality.
It's also the way to shut down debilitating self-
criticism, even when there is something to it.
For God is greater than our worried hearts and
knows more about us than we do ourselves.
And friends, once that's taken care of and we're
no longer accusing or condemning ourselves,
we're bold and free before God! We're able to
stretch our hands out and receive what we asked
for because we're doing what he said, doing what
pleases him. Again, this is God's command: to
believe in his personally named Son,
Jesus Christ. He told us to love each other,
in line with the original command. As we
keep his commands, we live deeply and
surely in him, and he lives in us. And this is
how we experience his deep and abiding
presence in us: by the Spirit he gave us.

1 JOHN 3:18–24 THE MESSAGE

Whatever you have learned or received or heard from me, or seen in me—put it into practice. And the God of peace will be with you.

Philippians 4:9 NIV

You will find as you look back upon your life, that the moments when you have really lived are the moments when you have done things in the spirit of love.

Henry Drummond

Always There

We need never shout across the spaces to an
absent God. He is nearer than our own soul,
closer than our most secret thoughts.

A. W. TOZER

God is always present in the temple of your
heart...His home. And when you come in to meet
Him there, you find that it is the one place of deep
satisfaction where every longing is met.

Always be in a state of expectancy, and see that
you leave room for God to come in as He likes.

OSWALD CHAMBERS

God is the sunshine that warms us, the rain
that melts the frost and waters the young plants.
The presence of God is a climate of strong
and bracing love, always there.

JOAN ARNOLD

*P*rayer is...an ever-available door by
which to come into God's presence.

*D*OUGLAS *V*. *S*TEERE

*M*y Presence will go with you,
and I will give you rest.

*E*XODUS 33:14 NIV

*T*here is nothing we can do that will make
God love us less, and there's nothing we can
do that will make Him love us more. He will
always and forever love us unconditionally.
What He wants from us is that we love
Him back with all our heart.

God's Love for Us

This is what real love is: It is not our love for God;
it is God's love for us. He sent his Son to die in our
place to take away our sins.
Dear friends, if God loved us that much we also should
love each other. No one has ever seen God,
but if we love each other, God lives in us,
and his love is made perfect in us.
We know that we live in God and he lives in us,
because he gave us his Spirit.... And so we know the
love that God has for us, and we trust that love.
God is love. Those who live in love live in God, and
God lives in them.... Where God's love is, there is no
fear, because God's perfect love drives out fear....
We love because God first loved us.

1 JOHN 4:10–13, 16, 18–19 NCV

Real love is always a gift from God: a gift of Himself.

EUGENIA PRICE

*B*ut God demonstrates his own love
for us in this: While we were still sinners,
Christ died for us.

*R*OMANS 5:8 NIV

*T*he God of the universe—the One who created
everything and holds it all in His hand—created each
of us in His image, to bear His likeness, His imprint.
It is only when Christ dwells within our hearts,
radiating the pure light of His love through our
humanity, that we discover who we are and what
we were intended to be.

Indescribable Love

Could we with ink the ocean fill,
And were the skies of parchment made,
Were every stalk on earth a quill,
And every man a scribe by trade
To write the love of God above
Would drain the ocean dry,
Nor could the scroll contain the whole
Though stretched from sky to sky.

MEIR BEN ISAAC NEHORAI

We are of such value to God that He came to live
among us...and to guide us home. He will go to any
length to seek us, even to being lifted high upon the
cross to draw us back to Himself. We can only respond
by loving God for His love.

CATHERINE OF SIENA

Though you have not seen him, you love him...and are
filled with an inexpressible and glorious joy.

1 PETER 1:8 NIV

*H*e has remembered his love and his
faithfulness...all the ends of the earth have
seen the salvation of our God.

*P*SALM 98:3 NIV

*G*od has put into each of our lives a void that cannot
be filled by the world. We may leave God or put Him
on hold, but He is always there, patiently waiting for
us...to turn back to Him.

*E*MILIE *B*ARNES

A New Song

Then GOD promises to love me all day, sing songs all
through the night! My life is God's prayer.

PSALM 42:8 THE MESSAGE

Your promises have been thoroughly tested;
that is why I love them so much.

PSALM 119:140 NLT

The LORD your God is with you, he is mighty to save.
He will take great delight in you, he will quiet you with
his love, he will rejoice over you with singing.

ZEPHANIAH 3:17 NIV

I would be always in the thick of life,
Threading its mazes, sharing its strife,
Yet—somehow singing!

ROSELLE MERCIER MONTGOMERY

*S*atisfy us in the morning
with your unfailing love,
that we may sing for joy
and be glad all our days.

*P*SALM 90:14 NIV

O sing unto the LORD a new song:
sing unto the LORD, all the earth.

*P*SALM 96:1 KJV

*T*he joyful birds prolong the strain,
their song with every spring renewed;
the air we breathe, and falling rain,
each softly whispers: God is good.

*J*OHN *H*AMPDEN *G*URNEY

The Heart of the Matter

In comparison with this big world, the human
heart is only a small thing. Though the world
is so large, it is utterly unable to satisfy this tiny
heart. Our ever-growing soul and its capacities
can be satisfied only in the infinite God.
As water is restless until it reaches its level,
so the soul has no peace until it rests in God.

SADHU SUNDAR SINGH

We sometimes fear to bring our troubles to God,
because they must seem so small to Him who sits on
the circle of the earth. But if they are large enough
to worry us and endanger our welfare, they are large
enough to touch His heart of love.

R. A. TORREY

*G*od is so big He can cover the whole
world with His love and so small
He can curl up inside your heart.

JUNE MASTERS BACHER

*W*hom have I in heaven but You?
And besides You, I desire nothing on earth.
My flesh and my heart may fail, but God is the
strength of my heart and my portion forever....
As for me, the nearness of God is my good;
I have made the Lord GOD my refuge.

PSALM 73:25–26, 28 NASB

*A*ll perfect gifts are from above
and all our blessings show
The amplitude of God's dear love
which any heart may know.

LAURA LEE RANDALL

Extravagant Love

Watch what God does, and then you do it,
like children who learn proper behavior from
their parents. Mostly what God does is love you.
Keep company with him and learn a life of love.
Observe how Christ loved us. His love was not
cautious but extravagant. He didn't love in order
to get something from us but to give everything
of himself to us. Love like that.

EPHESIANS 5:1–2 THE MESSAGE

To love by freely giving is its own reward.
To be possessed by love and to in turn give love
away is to find the secret of abundant life.

GLORIA GAITHER

Change your life.... Come back to God, your God.
And here's why: God is kind and merciful.
He takes a deep breath, puts up with a lot,
this most patient God, extravagant in love.

JOEL 2:13 THE MESSAGE

Love is extravagant in the price
it is willing to pay, the time it is willing
to give, the hardships it is willing to endure,
and the strength it is willing to spend.
Love never thinks in terms of "how little,"
but always in terms of "how much."
Love gives, love knows, and love lasts.

JONI EARECKSON TADA

*When we love someone, we want to be with them,
and we view their love for us with great honor
even if they are not a person of great status.
For this reason—and not because of our great status—
God values our love. So much, in fact,
that He suffered greatly on our behalf.*

JOHN CHRYSOSTOM

You Are Mine

Don't be afraid, I've redeemed you. I've called your
name. You're mine. When you're in over your head,
I'll be there with you. When you're in rough waters,
you will not go down. When you're between a rock
and a hard place, it won't be a dead end—because I
am GOD, your personal God, the Holy of Israel, your
Savior. I paid a huge price for you...! *That's* how much
you mean to me! *That's* how much I love you!

ISAIAH 43:1–4 THE MESSAGE

Our God is so wonderfully good, and lovely, and
blessed in every way that the mere fact of belonging to
Him is enough for an untellable fullness of joy!

HANNAH WHITALL SMITH

If God is for us, who can be against us?

ROMANS 8:31 NIV

Do not be afraid to enter the cloud that is settling
down on your life. God is in it. The other side is
radiant with His glory.

L. B. COWMAN

*B*ut let all who take refuge in you be glad; let them ever sing for joy. Spread your protection over them, that those who love your name may rejoice in you. For surely, O LORD, you bless the righteous; you surround them with your favor as with a shield.

*P*SALM 5:11–12 NIV

*Y*ou are valuable just because you exist. Not because of what you do or what you have done, but simply because you are. Just think about the way Jesus honors you...and smile.

*M*AX *L*UCADO

Peace and Harmony

Clothe yourselves with compassion, kindness, humility, gentleness and patience. Bear with each other and forgive whatever grievances you may have against one another. Forgive as the Lord forgave you. And over all these virtues put on love, which binds them all together in perfect unity. Let the peace of Christ rule in your hearts, since as members of one body you were called to peace. And be thankful.
Let the word of Christ dwell in you richly as you teach and admonish one another with all wisdom, and as you sing psalms, hymns and spiritual songs with gratitude in your hearts to God.

COLOSSIANS 3:12–16 NIV

May God, who gives this patience and encouragement, help you live in complete harmony with each other.

ROMANS 15:5 NLT

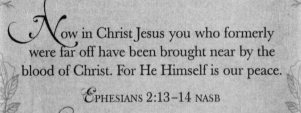

Now in Christ Jesus you who formerly
were far off have been brought near by the
blood of Christ. For He Himself is our peace.

EPHESIANS 2:13–14 NASB

Nothing can give you quite the same thrill
as the feeling that you are in harmony
with the great God of the universe
who created all things.

JAMES DOBSON

Love Letter

The work of creating is an act of love. The God
who flung from His fingertips this universe filled
with galaxies and stars, penguins and puffins...
peaches and pears, and a world full of children
made in His own image, is the God who loves
with magnificent monotony.

BRENNAN MANNING

All the things in this world are gifts and signs of God's
love to us. The whole world is a love letter from God.

PETER KREEFT

It is an extraordinary and beautiful thing that God, in
creation...works with the beauty of matter; the reality
of things; the discoveries of the senses, all five of them;
so that we, in turn, may hear the grass growing; see
a face springing to life in love and laughter.... The
offerings of creation...our glimpses of truth.

MADELEINE L'ENGLE

*I'm a little pencil in the hands of a loving God
who is writing a love letter to the world.*

MOTHER TERESA

*Let love and faithfulness never leave you;
bind them around your neck, write them
on the tablet of your heart.*

PROVERBS 3:3 NIV

*The reason for loving God is God Himself,
and the measure in which we should love
Him is to love Him without measure.*

BERNARD OF CLAIRVAUX

The Whole Truth

God wants us to grow up, to know the whole truth
and tell it in love–like Christ in everything. We take
our lead from Christ, who is the source of everything
we do. He keeps us in step with each other. His very
breath and blood flow through us, nourishing us so
that we will grow up healthy in God, robust in love.

EPHESIANS 4:15–16 THE MESSAGE

From the tiny birds of the air and from
the fragile lilies of the field we learn the same truth,
which is so important for those who desire a life
of simple faith: God takes care of His own.
He knows our needs. He anticipates our crises.
He is moved by our weaknesses. He stands ready
to come to our rescue. And at just the right
moment He steps in and proves Himself
as our faithful heavenly Father.

CHARLES SWINDOLL

Jesus said, "If you hold to my teaching, you are really my disciples. Then you will know the truth, and the truth will set you free."

JOHN 8:31–32 NIV

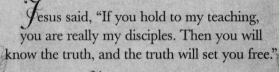

Lord, give me work to do; give me health;
Give me joy in simple things.
Give me an eye for beauty,
A mouth to speak truth,
and a heart full of love.

God Reaching Out

If we are children of God, we have a tremendous
treasure in nature and will realize that it is holy
and sacred. We will see God reaching out to us
in every wind that blows, every sunrise and sunset,
every cloud in the sky, every flower that blooms,
and every leaf that fades.

OSWALD CHAMBERS

The longer I live, the more my mind dwells upon
the beauty and the wonder of the world.

JOHN BURROUGHS

Look up at all the stars in the night sky and hear
your Father saying, "I carefully set each one
in its place. Know that I love you more than these."
Sit by the lake's edge, listening to the water
lapping the shore, and hear your Father gently
calling you to that place near His heart.

WENDY MOORE

The God who made the world and everything in it is the Lord of heaven and earth…. He himself gives all men life and breath and everything else…. God did this so that men would seek him and perhaps reach out for him and find him, though he is not far from each one of us. "For in him we live, and move, and have our being."

Acts 17:24–28 NIV

God has a wonderful plan for each person He has chosen. He knew even before He created this world what beauty He would bring forth from our lives.

Louis B. Wyly

He Loves to Listen

I love the LORD because he hears my voice and my prayer for mercy. Because he bends down to listen, I will pray as long as I have breath!

PSALM 116:1–2 NLT

Keep company with GOD, get in on the best.
Open up before GOD, keep nothing back;
he'll do whatever needs to be done: He'll validate
your life in the clear light of day and stamp
you with approval at high noon.

PSALM 37:4–6 THE MESSAGE

We do not know what we ought to pray for,
but the Spirit himself intercedes for us with groans
that words cannot express. And he who searches our
hearts knows the mind of the Spirit, because the Spirit
intercedes for the saints in accordance with God's will.
And we know that in all things God works for the
good of those who love him, who have been called
according to his purpose.

ROMANS 8:26–28 NIV

No matter where we are,
God can hear us from there!
He loves to hear our hearts' prayers
and draw near when we call to Him.

*Hear my cry, O God; give heed to
my prayer. From the end of the earth
I call to You when my heart is faint;
lead me to the rock that is higher than I.
For You have been a refuge for me.*

PSALM 61:1–3 NASB

An Invitation

If you have ever:

    questioned if this is all there is to life...

    wondered what happens when you die...

    felt a longing for purpose or significance...

    wrestled with resurfacing anger...

    struggled to forgive someone...

    known there is a "higher power" but

      couldn't define it...

    sensed you have a role to play in the world...

    experienced success and still felt empty afterward...

then consider Jesus.

A great teacher from two millennia ago, Jesus of Nazareth, freely chose to show our Maker's everlasting love for us by offering to take all of our flaws, darkness, and mistakes into His very body (1 Peter 2:24). The result was His death on a cross. But the story doesn't end there. God raised Him to newness of life, and invites us to believe this truth in our hearts and follow Jesus into eternal life.

If you confess with your mouth that Jesus is Lord and believe in your heart that God raised him from the dead, you will be saved. –ROMANS 10:9